I0483918

Direct-to-Consumer Advertisement (DTC):

How Pharmaceutical Companies Use Economic Modeling to Drive Up Prices on Your Medicines at the Pharmacy, Bring Great Prescriptions Drugs to the Market and Demonstrate the Value of Economic Mathematics to the Science of Advertising

By Timothy John Tucker

ISBN: **1508786631**
ISBN-13: **978-1508786634**

DEDICATION

This is a work of love - love for the industry that brings so many valuable products and services to human health and well-being. May it also serve to demonstrate a proof-of-principle: that small and tactical ideas firmly executed win against big ideas that are never executed.

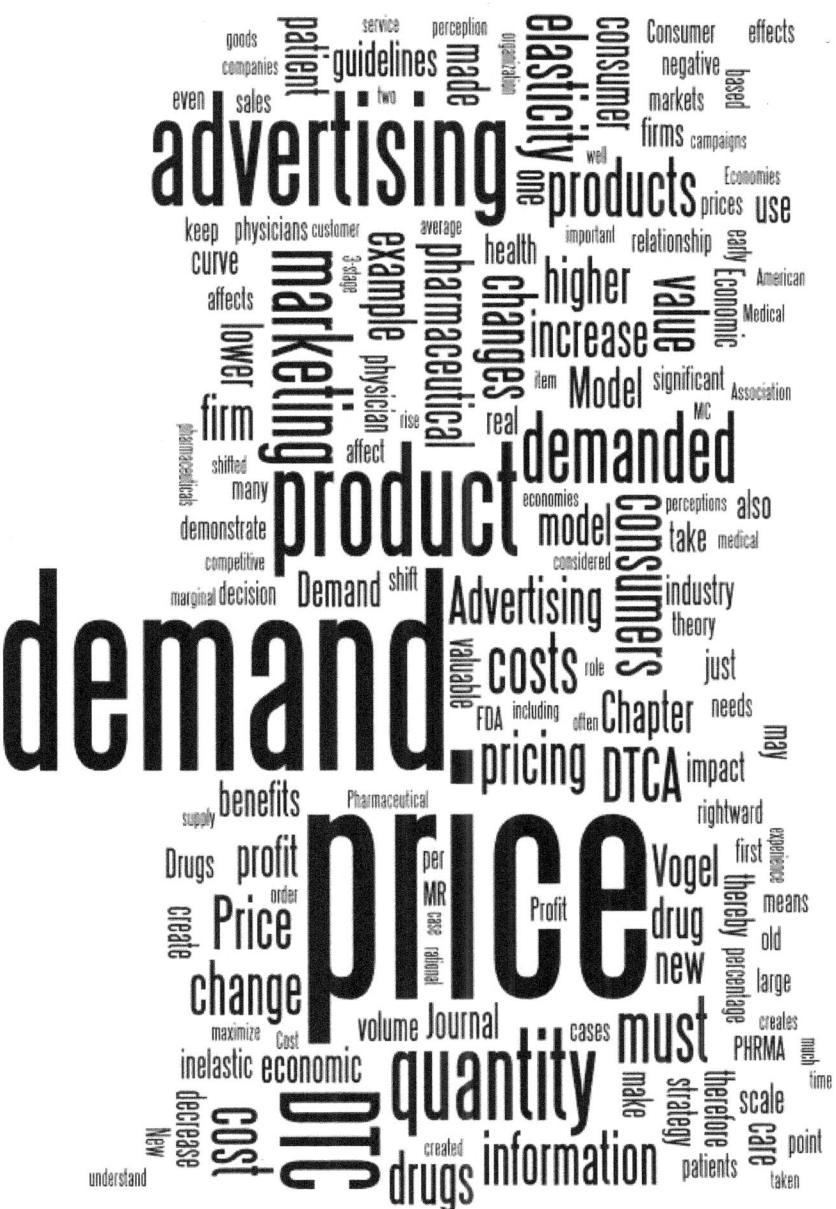

OTHER CO-AUTHORED
PUBLICATIONS
BY THE AUTHOR

Hamuro, L., Zhang, G., Tucker, T. J., Self, C., Strittmatter, W. J., & Burke, J. R. (2007). Optimization of a polyglutamine aggregation inhibitor peptide (QBP1) using a thioflavin T fluorescence assay. *Assay and drug development technologies*, *5*(5), 629-636.

Nagai, Y., Tucker, T., Ren, H., Kenan, D. J., Henderson, B. S., Keene, J. D., ... & Burke, J. R. (2000). Inhibition of polyglutamine protein aggregation and cell death by novel peptides identified by phage display screening. *Journal of Biological Chemistry*, *275*(14), 10437-10442.

Ren, H., Nagai, Y., Tucker, T., Strittmatter, W. J., & Burke, J. R. (2001). Amino acid sequence requirements of peptides that inhibit polyglutamine-protein aggregation and cell death. *Biochemical and biophysical research communications*, *288*(3), 703-710.

Lai, T. S., Tucker, T., Burke, J. R., Strittmatter, W. J., & Greenberg, C. S. (2004). Effect of tissue transglutaminase on the solubility of proteins containing expanded polyglutamine repeats. *Journal of neurochemistry*, *88*(5), 1253-1260.

Lai, T. S., Liu, Y., Tucker, T., Daniel, K. R., Sane, D. C., Toone, E., ... & Greenberg, C. S. (2008). Identification of chemical inhibitors to human tissue transglutaminase by screening existing drug libraries. *Chemistry & biology*, *15*(9), 969-978.

Timothy John Tucker

CONTENTS

ACKNOWLEDGMENTS

This book would not be possible without the diligent guidance by Professors Richard Kouri, PhD, Steve Schanz JD, and. Sam Straight (who knows as much as any PhD about Big Pharma). These fine gentlemen guided me in ways they cannot fully know while I was attending the North Carolina State University Poole College of Management and the North Carolina State University Jenkins MBA Program. Moreover, Mr. Paul Herzich and Ms. Kim Krynski (who graciously acquiesced to my desire to publish my personal portion of the joint graduate student project) have my sincere appreciation. I would have never had the time or willingness to pursue my studies at Jenkins, however, without the patience and understanding of my wife, Maria Tucker. I'm still figuring out how to merge my talents and interests – but I think I'm getting closer.

Those who may wish to observe the original work in a slideshow summary may visit my LinkedIn Profile (see end of this book) or visit SlideShare to see the project. I hope this is of help.

INTRODUCTION:

DTCA AT A GLANCE

As the medical field continues to evolve, the health care industry has taken on numerous challenges. Advertising for pharmaceuticals has shifted away from the more traditional route of marketing towards health care providers and instead towards marketing directly to consumers. This has led to challenges in the health care industry that had not been faced fully in the past. Some changes include: consumers being more aware of the drugs they are prescribed by physicians, more transparency in the benefits and risks associated with the drugs the consumer can take, and pushing the consumer to make certain choices in the prescribing of their own medications. *Pharmaceutical companies marketing their products spend millions of dollars annually to just make sure their consumers are aware of the benefits associated with the product they produce.* Through the use of historical information from the health care industry and key economic theory this book seeks to determine if and how this increased spending on marketing affects the price consumers must pay for their pharmaceutical needs.

This easy-to-read and to-the-point book is designed as a guide to practical application for marketing directors and decision-makers of small and mid-size pharmaceutical companies –mainly because 21st Century executives use data to drive their decisions. The concepts and applications, however, could be used for any information externality companies (such as IT) of any size and scope as well. Our findings provide evidence of a shift of the importance of information externalities today.

CHAPTER 1:

PERCEPTION

There is a public perception that large expenditures on advertising is wasteful and only raises the cost of drugs. These perceptions are based on the belief that drug firm products exist in perfectly competitive markets with perfect substitutes, that consumers have perfect information and that products are homogeneous.[1] In other words, these perceptions are not based on the real-world market. In addition, one of the errors committed in the past with Direct-to-Consumer campaigns has been that firms have failed to treat consumers as rational entities. It is this irrationality-perception, coupled with poor planning and/or strategy that has evoked perceptions of advertising cost failure. While popular drugs often incur higher prices, one must look to another model to make sense of the rise of DTC marketing interests.

Direct-to Consumer Advertising, interchangeably referred to as both DTCA and DTC, is the promotion of prescription drugs through newspaper, magazine, television and internet marketing.

Drug companies also produce other materials, including brochures and videos, that are available in doctors' offices or designed to be given to patients by medical professionals or via patient groups. There is a similar practice of sponsorship for large sporting events too, often seemingly unrelated to the event, but it often correlated with the target customer in attendance of the event.

For most new products, advertising is a cost that is necessary to create primary demand. Effective advertising creates an awareness of a product already priced at some point that reflects a reference value, along with positive and negative value additions. But pharmaceuticals are somewhat unusual in that they:

- are specialty experience goods
- are usually created by unique manufacturers
- always strategically use economies of scale
- have large startup costs
- benefit from *both* economies of scale *and* scope (not just one or the other)
- are information externalities.[2]

Pharmaceutical advertising-to-sales ratios are among the lowest for experience goods. In other words, compared to other experience goods (like beer, fast food, cosmetics and pet care products), *less is spent on advertising per unit*.[3] The pharmaceutical customer is in a position of incomplete information and therefore relies on external sources of credibility to derive value of the product. If a physician is quiet about a drug's effectiveness, the consumer relies on his/her

own perception of value. Because consumers are rational and understand that mass marketing campaigns are expensive, those products must therefore be valuable. There is significant research to show that DTC creates valuable *recall cues* that create a significant impact for consumers when it comes time to decide among competing products. In the U.S., doctors are not considered principal agents of the drugs and therefore consumers may rely more on information they receive outside the office if the physician doesn't bring up the subject. The consumer may then infer that valuable advertising means a valuable product. A greater incidence of advertising is a signal of both a quality item and a better buy.[4]

The point here is that advertising costs for DTC do not by themselves add significantly to the cost of a drug. The huge costs incurred to bring a drug to market overwhelmingly dwarf even large advertising budgets. While some minimal additional marketing costs are demand-variable, most advertising costs are sunk early in promotions phase.[5] One must dig deeper to see if there may be something more interesting at work.

CHAPTER 2

TRADITIONAL MODELS OF ADVERTISING

As early as the 19th century, advertising was under scrutiny. Alfred Marshall, the famed economist, related the distinction between roles of advertising. He stated that advertising is constructive when it provides wanted information with lowered costs for the product. He also stated that advertising is wasteful from a social perspective when it contains non-valuable information or only serves to redistribute consumption from one product to the next within the same class of product.[7]

Accordingly, there are two models justified. The first is the Market Power Model and is largely a tool of persuasion. The second model is the Information Model, of which the main premise is that advertising makes the consumer more aware of viable alternatives to existing conditions – thereby increasing the consideration set.

Timothy John Tucker

Interestingly, the Marketing Power Model is one in which price inelasticity plays an important role. Likewise, the caveat of the Information Model is that price differentiation may strengthen and thereby decrease price elasticity for the product.[8] With DTCA, the situation is more complex as neither model successfully creates an explainable cause for usage.

CHAPTER 3

A NEW MODEL FOR DTCA RATIONALITY: 3-STAGE COMPARATIVE ECONOMIC STATICS

Gonul, *et al* concluded that competitive marketing practices by pharmaceutical firms is mostly informative.[9] But information alone does not explain the variability of impact from campaign to campaign. In addition, the regulations by the FDA necessitate full disclosure of side effects. Information alone also does not explain the dramatic price elasticity of many pharmaceutical products. Therefore, a new model that can isolate the pieces of this puzzle is needed. This is where a 3-stage economic statics analysis becomes valuable. By individually analyzing such impacts as demand shifts, marginal costs and revenues, and average total costs can all play out their roles. Historically, a relatively small increase in DTCA spending results in dramatic shifts in demand rightward. Economies of scale allow the average total cost and the marginal revenue to shift upward

slightly. Figures 1 and 2 in the attached addendum contrast the impact of these three economic factors realign.

Robert Baukus states that "The basic strategy behind DTCA is to increase patient inquiries about advertised drugs and thereby create a positive force or "patient pull' to influence awareness and sales levels."[10] As Hollon puts it, "The principal effect of DTC marketing is to create consumer demand, changing the physician-patient relationship into a physician-consumer relationship."[11] This model also requires that consumers are cynical rationalists, that is they fully expect advertising to exclude information on side effects, inflate the benefits and cast doubt on competing brands.[12] That is, after all, how competitive capitalism works. It is this rational cynicism that helped to develop the 3-stage model. Vaithianathan even argues that DTCA is most effective when doctors are imperfect agents (and therefore not trusted by their patients) and that the rise of DTCA can be directly attributed to managed care pressure.[13]

CHAPTER 4

PRICE ELASTICITY OF DEMAND (PED)

Price elasticity of demand plays a huge role in the price setting decision making process. Price elasticity shows how much the demand for a product or service changes as the price changes. If quantity demanded does not change much when price changes than this is said to have an inelastic demand. If quantity demanded changes quite a bit as price changes than this product or service is considered to have a very elastic demand. If your product has a low elasticity, you can raise prices without worrying about how much this will affect your sales.

The price elasticity of demand for a good or service can be determined by first calculating the percentage change in quantity demanded. To do this you must subtract the old quantity demanded from the new quantity demanded, then divide that number over the

Timothy John Tucker

old quantity demanded. You must then find the percentage change in price. This is calculated by subtracting the old price from the new price, then dividing that number by the old price. You then divide the percentage change in quantity demanded by the percentage change in price and you have found the price elasticity of demand for the product. The lower the absolute value (take away the negative sign if the answer is negative) the more inelastic your demand is. We will demonstrate this formula in use below to make it easier to understand.

Old Price	New Price	Old Quant. Demand	New Quant. Demand	% Change Quant. Dem.	% Change in Price	PED
10	15	50	45	-0.1	0.5	-0.2
10	15	50	30	-0.4	0.5	-0.8

In this example we have two products, we can call the top product "A" and the bottom product "B". Both of these products originally sold for the same price and had the same change in price, yet their quantity demanded was affected differently. In both cases the quantity demanded dropped, but by differing amounts. As can be seen by the example above, the higher the absolute value of the price elasticity of demand the more a price change affects the quantity demanded. So product "A" effects a smaller decrease in quantity demanded, while product "B" effects a larger decrease in the quantity demanded. In the case of a price increase the more inelastic product made a higher profit, while the more elastic product demonstrates a decrease in profit.

CHAPTER 5

PRICING DECISIONS

We can take the theory of price elasticity of demand a step further and show the role it plays in how pharmaceutical companies set their prices using two distinct strategies. Whenever there is a shift in demand rightward, such as the case with DTC, there will be a choice that needs to be made by the firm: to price higher as the standard price-maximizing theory demands, or price lower as economies of scale allow, in order to maximize volume-derived profit. This decision should not be taken lightly, after all millions (or even billions of dollars) could be left on the table if the decision is made incorrectly.

Timothy John Tucker

Below is an example of a highly inelastic demand, which demonstrates the impact on profit.

Strategy	Quantity	Cost	Price	Profit	Total Profit
Normal	10	100	200	100	1000
DTC price	11	90	300	210	2310
DTC volume	15	90	180	90	1350

As can be seen by from this example, more profit can be created from pricing high under an inelastic demand. If the demand curve were more elastic, as can happen in extreme examples of over-saturation of markets, profitability changes. Such an example follows.

Strategy	Quantity	Cost	Price	Profit	Total Profit
Normal	10	100	200	100	1000
DTC price	8	90	300	210	1680
DTC volume	20	90	180	90	1800

In this case, where an increase in price does affect the quantity sold significantly, the choice would be to price lower, in order to maximize volume. Historically, the first example has dominated the pharmaceutical landscape.

Again, any shift in demand can create a similar effect. For example, an article in a reputable medical journal (such as the prestigious *Journal of the American Medical Association, JAMA*), demonstrating a true advantage in use of the therapy, can drive patient demand up. A

Timothy John Tucker

recommendation by a prominent physician's organization (such as the *American Medical Association, AMA*) can influence physicians to recommend it to patients, thereby driving up demand as well.

Alternatively, a press report in a prime time media broadcast (whether credible or not) portraying the safety or efficacy of a medication in a negative light can drastically lower demand for the product. The distinction is that DTC has the potential to be the most powerful tool available for the pharmaceutical company to *directly* drive demand at any point the firm chooses. All other examples are indirect means that carry significant inherent risk. DTC (if used with responsibility) can be tremendously useful and usually carries little risk of failure.

If it has not been clear before, the answer should be crystal clear now: historic unique pharmaceutical prices has been driven by the highly inelastic demand for these experience goods.

CHAPTER 6

CONSIDERATIONS ABOUT PRICING

What does this modeling mean to an executive who must make the decision for pricing? It means that cost-effectiveness must be below the threshold of willingness to pay. It means that the Value (price) should equal the reference price of the next best product or alternative multiplied by the perceived differentiation over the standard therapy. The executive should understand the potential tradeoff between a price that meets the internal rate of return on investment (or in some cases the internal rate of return) and the price that will be considered cost-effective by payers. Gut feelings are of no use here when the executive has to answer to his shareholders. But health economics (including a healthcare economic value add, or EVA) can demonstrate a more accurate pricing strategy.[14] The firm would ideally want to price anticipating this higher value perception and therefore might have to forego early DTCA in order to educate

the physicians and thereby "prime the pump" - fulfilling the informational component of advertising.

What kind of spending might we be talking about?

Rank	Media	US DTC media $ (millions)	% change vs. prior year
1	Television	$2,481.7	12.7%
2	Magazine	$1,085.8	6.6%
3	Newspaper	$149.2	-28.9%
4	Internet*	$59.8	-14.4%
5	Radio	$24.3	4.9%
6	Outdoor	$3.8	21.1%

DTC spend by media type, 2013

*Internet expenditures exclude all Yahoo! sites, Realtor.com, YouTube.com and MySpace.com

Source: Nielsen

Data from Nielsen shows generous pharmaceutical company expenditures during 2013. DTC spend across all media, excluding the Internet, rose 10%, from $3.4 billion in 2012 to just under $3.8 billion in 2013. Companies spent more in television ($2.48 billion, up 12.7% over the year-ago period), magazines ($1.09 billion, up 6.6%) and radio ($24.3 million, up 4.9%) than they did during 2012. The only declines were seen by newspapers ($149.2 million, down 28.9%) and the Internet ($59.8 million, down 14.4%).

{Source: Medical Marketing & Media, April 2014}

CHAPTER 7

RECOMMENDATIONS

The landscape of Direct to Consumer Advertising needs attention for any institution or individual wishing to navigate it, but there are certainly some take-home messages that have been described and should be taken to heart. The cumulative data behind such strategies that have historically been utilized successfully have been created using Big Data and sound economic theory.

The Top Ten keys to a winning DTC strategy are:

1. to follow the pricing guidelines set up by the industry organization PHRMA
2. use good common sense when applying those guidelines
3. decide early on the target customer the producing firm really wants
4. consider the complex ramifications of generics (based on the patent life), off-label competition and counterfeits

Timothy John Tucker

5. don't limit the offerings to the influencers (i.e. patients are not the real customers of the offering – the physician "buys" with a written prescription)
6. base pricing on economic analytical decisions suggested by the price elasticity models herein, then make the offering accordingly
7. keep relationships with physicians active (while following FDA rules of conduct) – the relationship between patient and physician is sacred and that relationship affects prescription-writing
8. keep up with PHRMA oversight to keep the practice legal for all firms as DTCA has been restricted - but not outlawed by federal regulations yet
9. Maintain high levels of doctor and education fitting patient safety and propriety, not just benefits of usage
10. Formulate a post-patent life pricing strategy well ahead of the patent expiration (perhaps progressively lowering) to keep generic competition at bay and keep supply high for patient access

PHRMA is a trade organization made up of experienced big pharmaceutical experts from different fields, but mainly consisting of marketing and business development gurus. It has vast resources that study many factors regarding drug marketing. These guidelines clearly lay out the facts that PHRMA has very carefully analyzed the data necessary for effective long-term advertising for highly branded firms. The guidelines deal with timing, education of physician and consumer, compliance with the FDA, truth in advertising, accountability and social responsibility. All these guidelines promote long-term and sustainable profitability for the firms. The guidelines also encourage feedback from the FDA, which should reduce questionable practices.[15]

Timothy John Tucker

Initiative client director, digital investment, Holly Dunn's advice to DTC pharma marketers hoping to stay ahead of the curve: improve your agility. "You have to be a little more cognizant of the possible constraints. You have to plan ahead and maintain flexibility in your plans," she explains. "It could take a while to get things approved; the regulatory feedback could vary or change. Something you think might go through quickly might not, so you either have to have a backup plan or you're going to go dark, and not by choice." *Initiative* is a global communications network within *IPG Mediabrands*, one of the world's preeminent media services entities and part of *Interpublic Group* (NYSE: IPG).

Strikeforce Communications founder and CEO Mike Rutstein, on the other hand, looks for new blood, namely the consumer goods business. "You have to bring new people into the fold who don't think the way that everybody else does," he says bluntly. "For DTC right now, it's a perfect storm. There's a heightened regulatory environment, there are products that don't always have demonstrable separation from one another and there are people on the client side that come from a background where product features and attributes are what's for sale. Given all that, it's no wonder there's so much pushback." *Strikeforce* is a communications company that specializes in Healthcare marketing in the nutraceutical, OTC, pharmaceutical, biotech and medical device space.

REFERENCES

[1] Mansfield, E. *Microeconomics.* 9th edition. New York: W. W. Norton and Co.; 1997:167-170.

[2] E.R. Berndt , R. S. Pindyke , P. Azoulay. *Consumption Externalities and Diffusion in Pharmaceutical Markets: Antiulcer Drugs.* Journal of Industrial Economics, Vol. 51, p. 243, June 2003

[3] Vogel R., Ramachandradran S., Zachry W. *A Three-Stage Model for Assessing the Probable Economic Effects of Direct-to-Consumer Advertising of Pharmaceuticals.* Clinical Therapeutics, Vol. 25; 2003: No.1: p. 315

[4] Vogel, p. 315

[5] Vogel, p. 320

[6] Vogel, p. 325

[7] Vogel, p 312

[8] Vogel, p.312-314

[9] Gonul F., Carter F., Petrova E., Srinivasan K. *Promotion of Prescription Drugs and Its Impact on Physician Choice Behavior.* Journal of Marketing. 2001; 65:79-90

[10] Baukus R. *DTC Advertising.* Journal of Health Communications. 2004; 9:563

[11] Hollon. MF. *Direct to Consumer Marketing of Prescription Drugs: Creating Consumer Demand.* Journal of the American Medical Association 1999; 281:382-4

[12] Vaithianathan R. *Better the Devil You Know that the Doctor You Don't: Is Advertising Drugs to Doctors More Harmful than Advertising to Patients?* Journal of Health Services Research & Policy. 2006; Vol.11 No.4: p. 236.

[13] Ibid.

[14] Stagginus U, Russell S. Friedman, Y (editor) *Maximizing the Strategic Impact of Health- and Pharmacoeconomics in Biotechnology Companies* Best Practices in Biotechnology Business Development Logos Press, Washington DC. 2008; 150-151

[15] http://www.phrma.org/files/DTCGuidingprinciples.pdf

APPENDIX

The Economic Realities

Inelastic demand curves are typical of most pharmaceuticals in the US. [[6] Vogel, p. 325] It is this highly inelastic demand curve that has predetermined the high costs of unique pharmaceuticals historically.

A higher price simply does not grossly affect demand, *at least in the short term*. No significant price change will affect drug sales. Again, the phrase *in the short term* is important because part of this system is inherent in the fact that 20-year patent protection (in the US) *guarantees* all pricing is for the short-term.

Also, unlike other markets where more competition exists, the price-optimizing strategy must be calculated where Marginal Cost equals Marginal Revenue. The intersections of supply curve and demand curve only demonstrate the absence of the Economic Value of noncompetitive drugs. If drug prices become regulated in the US in the future, this intersection will become even more important. In

Timothy John Tucker

such a scenario, demand is unlikely to increase (due to fewer sales and marketing promotions) and supply will only be enough to meet the minimal demand of the uninformed population and no more. In such cases, shortages are likely. Therefore, the only real possible outcome to avoid shortages would be for the government to begin price support systems such as *cost-plus pricing or guaranteed volume purchases*. Interestingly, such an increase in (potentially artificial) demand would result in the same kind of phenomenon as the DTC-derived demand increase!

The reality of the existence of expanding markets for new drugs (otherwise unrecognized demand), shifts the demand curve rightward. In so doing, we at first immediately see that there is a slight rise in marginal cost, but effectively no change in average total cost. But more interestingly, we see that the new quantity correlates with the rightward shifted demand curve, resulting in a higher price. There is an overall lower cost for production (lower ATC intersection with the new quantity), which benefits the firm as well. The impact derived between Figures 1 and 2 should demonstrate that there is a very real reason that DTC is desired by producers. It yields very real results at least in some cases. Importantly, we must concede that these benefits will most likely be short-lived for our example.

Timothy John Tucker

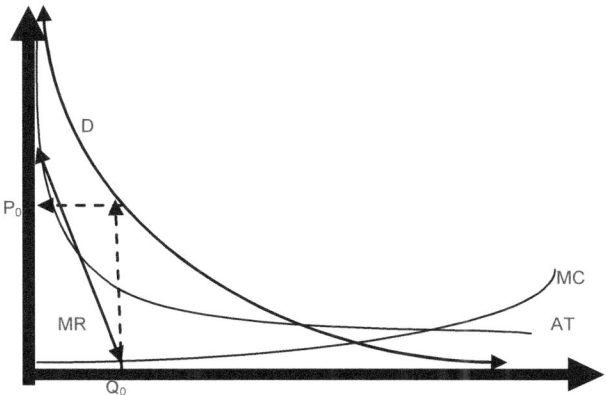

Figure 1. Classic Economic Model of Non-Competitive Goods. Typical of Monopoly power of Patented Drugs. Optimal Q is where MR=MC, correlating to Demand

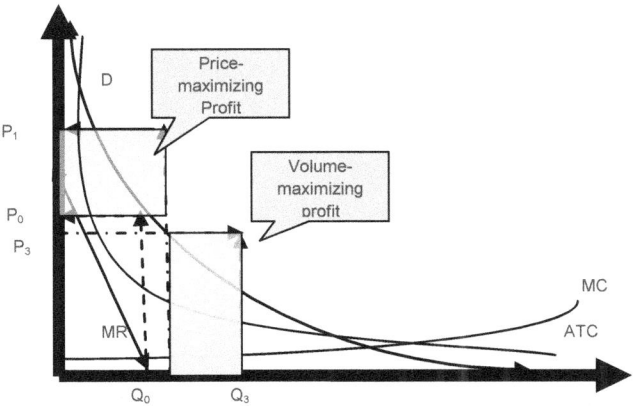

Figure 2. What Actually Happens When Firms Utilize DTCA. Demand, ATC and MR shift. Optimal Price is still where MR=MC, but MR and MC have shifted. Firm must choose between maximizing profit or delivering consumer-based value.

Timothy John Tucker

Seven Cautions regarding this model:

A reality check needs to be made here. We have made some assumptions that are not normally observed within a real world context:

1. a one-product company producing only one drug at a time
2. the firm seeks to maximize profits only
3. demand is the only factor for pricing
4. there are no price controls
5. there are no negotiations for volume, etc.
6. no supplier or distributor affects pricing
7. no differences have been made between disease state or product awareness campaigns

Economies of Scale:

Economies of scale take place when a firm can decrease costs on a per item basis by increasing the production of that item. This can take place for several reasons including technology advances, knowledge gaining or input costs. Let's say you own a company that builds cars. One of your inputs for the vehicles would be windshield wipers. You would purchase these windshield wipers from a separate manufacturer who may sell to you at a lower per unit cost if you buy in larger quantities. Decreasing your cost per unit allows you to increase your profit while maintaining the same selling price point. This is done within the healthcare industry through multiple allowing for higher economy of scales than can be seen in other industries.

Timothy John Tucker

ABOUT THE AUTHOR

Timothy John Tucker's passion is uncovering and taking advantage of market opportunities. Currently an author of 6 prestigious biotech R&D journal articles, he spent 17 years of his life in the pre-clinical discovery phase of neurodegenerative and pulmonary biomedical research for Duke University Medical Center and the balance working in personal sales and innovative marketing for various large companies such as Morgan Stanley Smith Barney, AIG, AXA Equitable, H.H.Gregg and Cisco Systems. His unique style and go-to-market strategies have earned him the reputation as a "shock and awe guerilla marketer." He earned a B.S. in Biological Sciences, a technology commercialization internship, and his MBA in BioPharma Management and Entrepreneurship from North Carolina State University. He currently volunteers to help professionals fulfill their dreams through skill development and character identification by engaging in open speaker forums and networking sessions in the Research Triangle Park (Morrisville), North Carolina.

Twitter: @timothyjtucker   Motivational Practice and Education
                @ioe_bio   The Internet of Everything Biotech

LinkedIn: http://www.linkedin.com/in/timothyjtucker

www.ingramcontent.com/pod-product-compliance
Lightning Source LLC
Chambersburg PA
CBHW070232210526
45168CB00020B/2085